This book belongs to

Justine Adkins
_____

_____

To Penny

(fabulous Godmother)

L.P.

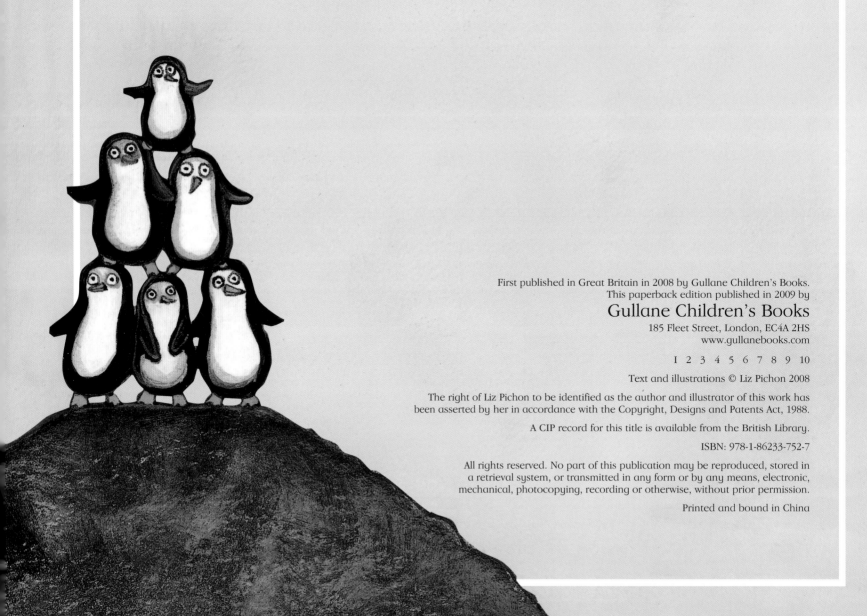

First published in Great Britain in 2008 by Gullane Children's Books.
This paperback edition published in 2009 by

Gullane Children's Books

185 Fleet Street, London, EC4A 2HS
www.gullanebooks.com

I 2 3 4 5 6 7 8 9 10

Text and illustrations © Liz Pichon 2008

The right of Liz Pichon to be identified as the author and illustrator of this work has
been asserted by her in accordance with the Copyright, Designs and Patents Act, 1988.

A CIP record for this title is available from the British Library.

ISBN: 978-1-86233-752-7

Printed and bound in China

Penguins

Liz Pichon

GULLANE
CHILDREN'S BOOKS

It's morning at the zoo.
The penguins wake up and have their first swim.
Penguins tend to do the same thing every day.

Here is a list of...
What Penguins Like To Do The Most.

1. Swim

2. Eat fish
(Fast - before the seagulls pinch them)

3. Play penguin games

4. Sleep standing up

5. Look at the people outside

6. Look at the people through the glass

Most days, nothing very exciting happens.

But today, it's a completely different story . . .

Little Penguin sees
something on the rock.

"DON'T TOUCH IT!"
says Big Penguin. "It belongs
to a person and they'll come
back to find it.

But nobody comes back.
So the penguins move closer for a better look.

"Is it food?" asks Hungry Penguin.
"I don't think so," says Big Penguin.
"It's a camera," Little Penguin squeaks.
"What do you do with a camera?" they ask.
"You smile at it!" grins Little Penguin.

"Are you sure you can't eat it?" asks Hungry Penguin.

"Let's press ALL the buttons!" says Bouncy Penguin, jumping on the camera.

FLASH!

It goes off.

"I DON'T LIKE IT!" cries Big Penguin. "Chill out!" says Little Penguin.

They peer through the camera lens.
"It's **too freaky**," says Big Penguin.

Little Penguin takes the camera.
"Hey everyone, look at me and say FISH!"

CLICK!

Now all the penguins
want to use the camera.

CLICK!

They take lots and lots
of fabulous pictures.

flash!

But suddenly...

. . . the camera stops working!

"Oh dear," says Big Penguin, "we'd better put it back."

So Little Penguin puts the camera back on the rock where he found it.

In the morning, the keeper finds the camera. "I'd better get this to *Lost Property* before those hungry penguins get their beaks on it!"

A little girl comes to collect her lost camera.

"Thank you!" she says excitedly.
"I can't wait to see all the
pictures I took at the zoo!"

There are pictures of monkeys, lions, tigers
and elephants. And, strangely, there are
quite a few pictures of penguins too!